sweet treats

to make, decorate, and give

sweet treats

to make, decorate, and give

Over 35 step-by-step recipes for making
and decorating cakes, cookies, and candies

Laura Tabor

CICO BOOKS

LONDON NEW YORK

I would like to dedicate this book to my very own bun in the oven that I am currently cooking, who has kept me company throughout this whole project!

Published in 2011 by CICO Books
An imprint of Ryland Peters & Small Ltd
20-21 Jockey's Fields   519 Broadway, 5th Floor
London WC1R 4BW   New York, NY 10012

www.cicobooks.com

10 9 8 7 6 5 4 3 2 1

Text © Laura Tabor 2011
Design and photography © CICO Books 2011

ISBN: 978 1 907563 07 2

Printed in China

Editor: Katie Hardwicke
Designer: Luis Peral-Aranda
Photographer: Stuart West
Styling and photographic art direction: Luis Peral-Aranda

CICO BOOKS
LONDON NEW YORK

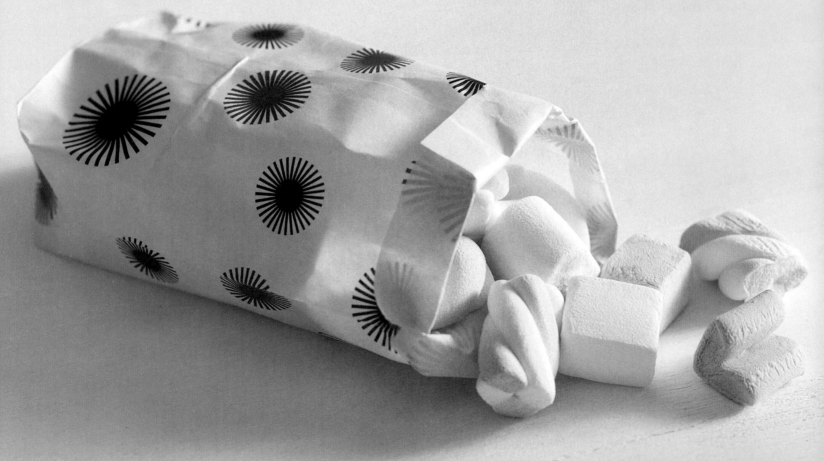

Contents

Introduction

From a young age I have always been a devotee of both baking and jewelry. As a child I would spend many happy hours cooking with my mother, who is an exceptional baker, but I also loved looking through her jewelry box and admiring her gorgeous collection. In time I decided my immediate future lay with jewelry and off I went to study jewelry design at London's Central St. Martin's College. But I never forgot about the time I spent in the kitchen, and cake baking always remained my therapeutic pleasure, helping relieve some of the stresses of study.

In 2001 I started my own jewelry label; designing, making, and selling my collections to boutiques and department stores around the world, which meant the time available to bake became less and less frequent. Luckily, a recent move to a beautiful new house complete with an amazing kitchen and a boyfriend with a big appetite meant my baking and candy-making passions were reignited. Then in 2010 I designed a jewellery collection entitled "Sweet," which was a range of "pic 'n' mix" candy-inspired silver and gold pieces. This was the first time that I had combined two of my great loves. After this it suddenly hit me that if I can make jewelry that looks like candy, then perhaps I can make confection that looks like jewelry! And so this is where my "Sweet Treats" journey began.

I hope you enjoy making and eating these delicious treats as much as I did writing this book. I'm sure you'll agree: they look good enough to wear!

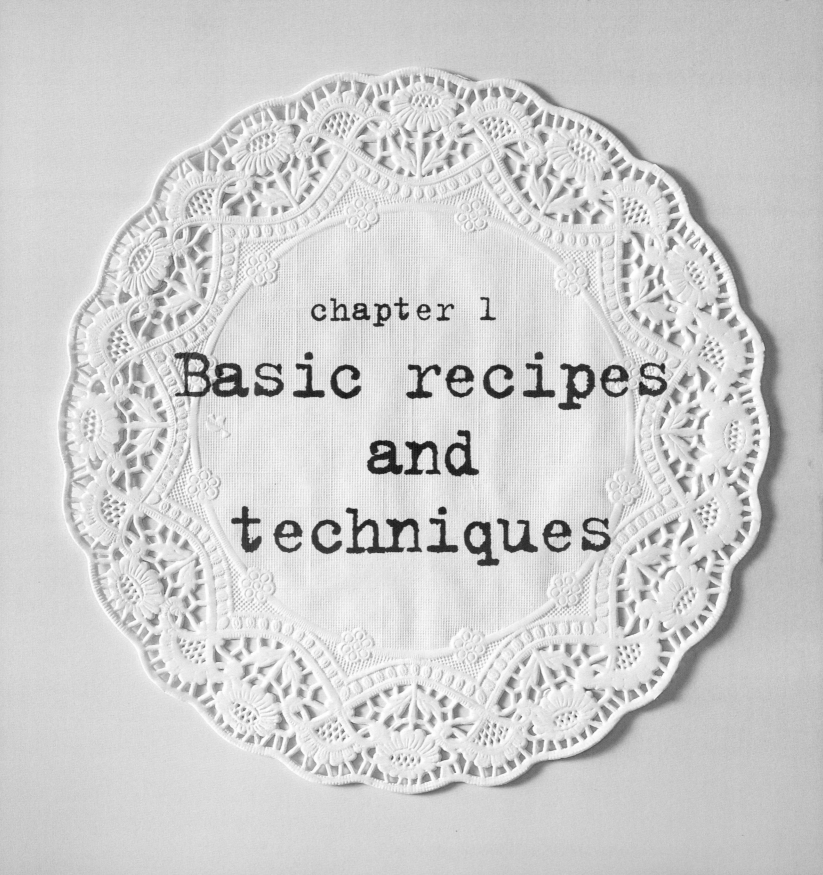

chapter 1

Basic recipes and techniques

equipment

There's a seemingly endless amount of kitchen utensils you can buy, but here are a few items that are used regularly throughout the book and will come in handy for any future baking projects.

A few basic items every baker should have are a rolling pin, beater, sieve, and measuring pitcher. A selection of spoons in different sizes is also useful for various tasks, such as stirring and spreading icing.

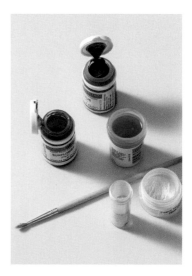

Paintbrushes and plastic nozzle bottles are ideal for adding decorative details and filling molds. Pastry brushes are another great tool to have to hand.

Cupcake cups come in all sorts of finishes that really help your cakes stand out.

Food coloring and edible glue are great to have to hand for coloring icing and adding decorative touches to your finished treats.

Cookie cutters are available in many different shapes and sizes, from simple circles to stars, hearts, numbers, and more.

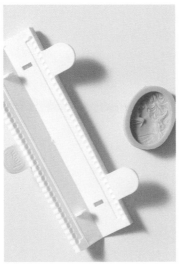

Use molds to make shapes from fondant icing. The one shown above will make a pretty string of small fondant pearls.

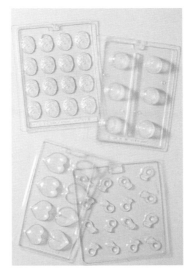

Molds come in all shapes and sizes and provide an easy way to make ornate candy, chocolates, and more. If you are working with hard candy make sure you choose a mold that is suited to the task.

Make lollipops using molds with special cavities to fit the lollipop sticks, which are readily available from craft stores.

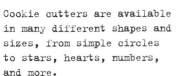

Edible pearls and jewels are perfect for adding that eyecatching finishing touch to your cookies or candy.

Presentation is all important when giving your sweet treats as gifts, so think about investing in some pretty doillies to display your creations on.

Craft stamps and punches can be bought in a host of designs and are perfect when working with rice paper.

A candy thermometer is a very useful purchase if you plan to try several of the recipes that involve working with heated sugar.

vanilla cupcakes

1 Preheat the oven to 350°F (180°C), Gas 4 and line a large or mini muffin pan with cupcake cups.

2 Put the butter and sugar in a bowl or food processor and beat on medium speed for a couple of minutes until creamy.

5 Remove from the oven and leave in the pan on a cooling rack for 2-3 minutes. Take out and let cool on the rack.

You will need:

- 1⅓ cups (300g) butter, softened
- 1½ cups (300g) superfine (caster) sugar
- 6 eggs
- 2¾ cups (300g) self-rising flour, sifted
- 2 tsp vanilla extract

Makes 24 medium-sized cupcakes or 40 mini cupcakes

3 Slowly beat in the eggs one at a time, continue to mix and add the vanilla extract when combined. Slowly add the flour.

4 Put an even amount of batter into each cup and put in the oven. For medium cakes, bake for 18 minutes or until springy and golden. For mini cupcakes bake for 8-10 minutes.

lemon variation

Follow the recipe above but add the grated zest of two lemons.

blueberry variation

Follow this recipe but add ¾ cup (150g) blueberries.

storage:

Cupcakes can be stored in a sealed container for up to a week or frozen for up to one month in an airtight container.

chocolate cupcakes

You will need:

- 1⅓ cups (300g) butter, softened
- 1½ cups (300g) superfine (caster) sugar
- 6 eggs
- 2 tsp vanilla extract
- 2½ cups (280g) self-rising flour, sifted
- 6 tbsp cocoa powder

Makes 24 medium-sized cupcakes or 40 mini cupcakes

1 Preheat the oven to 350°F (180°C), Gas 4 and line a large or mini muffin pan with cupcake cups.

2 Put the butter and sugar in a bowl or food processor and beat on medium speed for a couple of minutes until creamy.

3 Slowly beat in the eggs one at a time. Continue to mix and add the vanilla extract when combined. Slowly add the sifted flour and cocoa powder.

4 Using two spoons, put an even amount of batter into each cup and put in the oven. For medium cakes, bake for 18 minutes or until springy to the touch. For mini cakes bake for 8-10 minutes.

5 Remove from the oven and leave in the pan on a cooling rack for 2-3 minutes, then take out and let cool on the rack.

storage:
Cupcakes can be stored in a sealed container for up to one week or frozen for up to one month in an airtight container.

vanilla cake

1 Preheat the oven to 350°F (180°C), Gas 4. Butter a 9in (23cm) square cake pan and lightly dust with flour.

2 Cream the butter and sugar together in a mixing bowl by hand or in a food processor until fluffy.

3 Slowly beat in the egg yolks and eggs one at a time, until creamy and thoroughly combined. Slowly add the sifted flour, salt, and baking powder. Continue to beat for a few minutes then add the milk and vanilla extract. Stir until well mixed.

4 Pour the batter into the prepared pan. Run a knife through to remove any bubbles and tap gently. Bake for 40 minutes until golden and springy. Leave the cake in the pan for 15 minutes before turning out and leaving to cool completely. If required, use a cookie cutter to cut out shapes for the cakes.

You will need:

- 1 cup (250g) unsalted butter, softenend
- Heaped 1½ cups (310g) granulated sugar
- 2 large egg yolks
- 3 large eggs
- 2½ cups (250g) all-purpose (plain) flour, sifted
- ½ tsp salt
- 1½ tsp baking powder
- ½ cup (125ml) milk
- 2½ tsp vanilla extract

melting chocolate and filling molds

How to melt chocolate

You will need:
- Double boiler or bain marie
- Candy thermometer
- Wooden spoon

The best way to melt chocolate is in a double boiler or bain marie; this can be made by putting a heatproof bowl over a pan of gently simmering water. Make sure that the bottom of the bowl does not touch the water. It is also important to temper the chocolate to make it look glossy when it has been turned out of the molds.

1 Break up the chocolate pieces and put them in the heatproof bowl over the gently simmering water.

2 Let the chocolate begin to melt and when it has almost melted, stir it well. Heat dark chocolate to around 115°F (46°C,) and milk and white chocolate to 110°F (43°C).

3 Take the chocolate off the heat and remove the bowl of chocolate from the water bath. Stir continuously to temper the chocolate until it cools to around 85–90°F (29–32°C), this will ensure the chocolate tempers correctly which will give it a lovely glossy finish. It is ideal to keep the chocolate around this temperature when filling molds.

How to fill a chocolate mold

1 For projects using two different colored chocolates to provide detail, use a small paintbrush or a narrow tipped nozzle bottle to fill in the detailed area of the mold. Tap the mold to make sure you distribute the chocolate evenly.

2 Put the mold into the fridge until the detail is set, then fill the rest of the mold with the second color of chocolate. You can use a teaspoon or a plastic nozzle bottle.

3 Tap the mold gently to release any bubbles and to flow the chocolate evenly. Refrigerate the chocolates for at least 1 hour or until firmly set.

4 To release the chocolates, hold the mold upside down and gently push the chocolates out—they should drop out very easily, and if they do not then they are not yet cool enough.

You will need:
- Melted chocolate
- Small paintbrushes
- Plastic nozzle bottles
- Chocolate mold

gold dusting techniques

gold dusting chocolate

1 Use a small amount of edible glue on a paintbrush and paint a very thin layer onto the chocolate.

2 Use a clean, dry paintbrush and gently dab on the gold luster to the wet glue. Leave the chocolates to dry.

You will need:
- Clean dry paintbrushes
- Edible glue
- Edible gold luster

gold dusting sugar paste

1 Using a small paintbrush, paint a thin layer of edible gilding medium onto the sugar paste.

You will need:
- Clean dry paintbrushes
- Edible gilding medium
- Edible gold luster

2 Use a clean, dry paintbrush with a small amount of gold luster and gently dab it onto the sugar paste.

sugar paste icing

Sugar paste icing is great for covering cookies and cakes and is easy to mold into shapes. You can make different colors to suit your project.

You will need:

- 3¾ cups (500g) confectioners' (icing) sugar
- 1 egg white
- 2 tbsp liquid glucose
- Food coloring

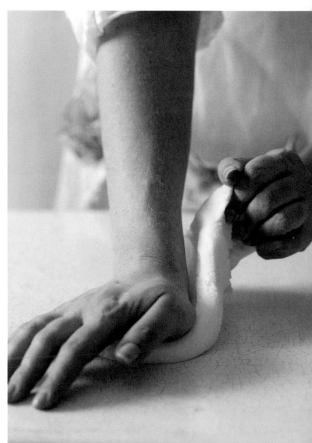

2 The paste will become very stiff and you should be able to roll it into a ball.

1 Sift the confectioners' (icing) sugar into a large bowl. Slowly add the egg white and liquid glucose and stir until combined into a dough.

3 Dust your work surface with confectioners' sugar and knead the paste lightly until it becomes smooth. Add more confectioners' sugar if it is too sticky.

4 At this stage you can add a little food coloring with a toothpick.

5 Knead the paste until the color is uniformly distributed.

6 Wrap the sugar paste tightly in plastic wrap to store. You can keep the sugar paste in the fridge for up to 4 weeks—make sure it is very tightly wrapped to avoid it drying out.

basic royal icing

Royal icing is used for lots of cookies and cake decoration. It can be piped on to provide detail and used to cover a whole cookie as a canvas for decoration.

1 Sift the confectioners' (icing) sugar into a large bowl. Slowly add the egg white and thoroughly mix together—don't pour all the egg in otherwise the icing will become dull. Keep mixing until the icing is glossy and has a consistency of thick heavy (double) cream. Add 2-3 drops of lemon juice. Keep the icing covered with plastic wrap or a damp cloth while you work with it, to prevent it drying out. The icing will keep for a few days if wrapped well in plastic wrap or kept in an airtight container.

2 You can color your basic royal icing with food coloring. I use pastes as it is easy to control the color and amount added. Whether using a paste or liquid, always start with a tiny bit on a toothpick— you can always add more and some colors are stronger than others. The colored icing can now be spooned into prepared piping bags for adding detailed decoration. If you are flooding the cookies (see below), save some of the colored icing in a bowl as you will need a separate consistency for this technique.

Flooding royal icing

"Flooding" is the technique used to cover a cookie in icing. It is simply royal icing that has been watered down slightly to a more runny consistency.

1 After you have made an outline on your cookie with the piped royal icing and it has dried it is time to "color in" your cookie with royal icing. Just add a few drops of water to the icing until it is as runny as light (single) cream. If it becomse too runny just add a little more confectioners' sugar.

2 You can use a teaspoon to flood the icing, but it is much easier to control with a plastic nozzle bottle. These are also a good way to store your icing. You can give the cookies a little tap to smooth the icing out to make a lovely flat surface and pop any air bubbles with a toothpick.

You will need:
- 3¾ cups (500g) confectioners' (icing) sugar
- 2 egg whites
- A few drops of lemon juice
- Food coloring

storage:
You can keep the royal icing in an airtight container for one week in the fridge.

buttercream icing

Basic buttercream icing

1 Put the butter in a large bowl or food processor. Sift the confectioners' (icing) sugar into the bowl and mix together until fluffy.

2 Add the milk and stir until completely combined and creamy.

3 Add a few drops of your chosen food coloring and ½ teaspoon of flavoring, if desired. Continue to mix until the color is even.

You will need:

- ½ cup (125g) unsalted butter, softened
- 2 cups (250g) confectioners' (icing) sugar
- 2 tbsp milk
- Food coloring

FLAVORING (optional):

- Rose water
- Orange flower water
- Almond essence
- Vanilla extract

storage:

The icing will keep in the fridge for up to 2 weeks in an airtight container). Remove from the fridge an hour or so before using to bring to room temperature.

Rich chocolate buttercream icing

1 Put the softened butter in a large bowl or food processor. Sift over the confectioners' (icing) sugar and cocoa powder and mix together until fluffy.

2 Melt the chocolate in a bain marie (see page 18) and let cool.

3 Add the cream and corn (golden) syrup to the melted chocolate and stir until combined.

4 Pour the chocolate mix into the buttercream and mix together until creamy and completely combined.

You will need:
- ½ cup (125g) butter
- 1¾ cups (225g) confectioners' (icing) sugar
- 4 tbsp cocoa powder
- 2 tbsp (40g) light corn syrup
- Scant 1 cup (200ml) light (single) cream
- 7oz (200g) dark chocolate

Lemon and cream cheese buttercream icing

1 Put the butter and cream cheese in a large bowl or food processor.

2 Sift over the confectioners' (icing) sugar and mix until fluffy.

3 Add the lemon juice and zest and continue to mix until creamy and completely combined.

You will need:
- Scant ½ cup (100g) butter, softened
- Scant ½ cup (100g) cream cheese
- 2⅓ cups (300g) confectioners' (icing) sugar
- 1½ tsp lemon juice
- Grated zest of 1 lemon

inverted sugar

Inverted sugar is a liquid form of sugar, which is required when making the marshmallow mixture for the pearls on page 48.

1 Put the sugar, ¾ cup (185ml) water, and lemon juice in a heavy bottomed saucepan.

2 Stir continuously and bring to a boil. Simmer at a low temperature for 20 minutes and stir occasionally.

3 Transfer into a glass jar with a lid. Once it has cooled it can be stored in the fridge for upto three weeks.

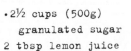

You will need:

- 2½ cups (500g) granulated sugar
- 2 tbsp lemon juice

❧

chapter 2

Beautiful treats for girls

jelly emeralds

These stunning jelly gems catch the light and trick your eyes. Serve the glamorous wobbly treats in a bowl with ice cream or just enjoy them on their own.

You will need:

- 3½oz (100g) or 8 cubes flavored Jell-o (jelly)
- 2 tbsp gelatin powder
- Food coloring (optional)

EQUIPMENT
- Heatproof pitcher
- Gem candy mold

1 Put the Jell-o, gelatin, and 1 cup cold water into a saucepan and heat gently, stirring continually until all the gel has dissolved. At this stage you can add a little extra color, if you like. Use a toothpick and mix in thoroughly. Pour into a heatproof pitcher and let cool for 5 minutes, making sure any bubbles have disappeared.

2 Carefully pour into the molds. If you use plastic nozzle bottles it will be easier to fill smaller and fiddly molds. Fill the molds right to the top, which makes removing them much easier. Leave the gems to cool for 10 minutes then put in the freezer until set for a further 10 minutes or so. Turn out the gems and enjoy!

Makes 6 large jelly gems or 12 small ones

tip:
You can make any kind of gem: use strawberry Jell-o for rubies; blackcurrant for amethyst; and lime or lemon for emerald variations. The choice is endless!

pearl shell candy lollies

These ocean-inspired glassy and glamorous pearl lollipops for grown-ups make a chic idea for a gift or to adorn a table at a party, individually wrapped in bags with beautiful ribbons or sitting in cute cups with sandy-looking sugar.

You will need:

- 1 cup (225g) granulated sugar
- 5 tbsp light corn syrup
- Large edible pearls

EQUIPMENT
- Shell lollipop hard candy mold
- Lollipop sticks
- Candy thermometer
- Toothpick
- Greased heatproof pitcher

1 Lightly butter the candy mold and put the lollipop sticks in place. Set to one side. Have your edible pearls and toothpick at the ready, too.

2 Put the sugar, ½ cup (125ml) water, and corn syrup into a heavy bottomed pan and stir to combine. Clip on a candy thermometer and begin to heat. Heat the sugar until it reaches 275°F (135°C). Do not let the temperature rise above this, otherwise your clear candy will become yellow.

3 As soon as the liquid reaches the correct temperature, transfer the mix into a greased heatproof pitcher, let the bubbles subside a little, then slowly pour a small amount into each cavity. Work quickly, as you don't have long before the mix begins to harden.

4 Drop a pearl onto each lolly and dip it into the middle of the candy shell with a toothpick. Let the lollies set for at least an hour. Turn them out onto waxed paper and store in an airtight container on waxed paper or dust lightly with cornflour to prevent sticking. Makes 5 lollipops

crystal cupcakes

These sparkling, crunchy crystal-topped cupcakes are ideal at a tea party and make a stunning gift for girls. The rock candy can be dyed various colors to look like your favorite semiprecious gemstones.

You will need:

- Rock sugar crystals
- Food coloring in assorted gem colors
- 1 quantity Lemon and Cream Cheese Buttercream (page 24)
- 1 quantity Lemon Cupcakes (page 13)

EQUIPMENT
- Palette knife

1 Make a batch of 12 Lemon Cupcakes (see page 13). While the cakes are cooling, put the rock sugar into separate bowls and add a small amount of different food coloring to each. Mix well with a small spoon until they look like semiprecious gems. Leave the crystals to dry for about 30 minutes.

2 Put the Lemon and Cream Cheese Buttercream into separate bowls for coloring. Add a small amount of food coloring to each batch. I like purple for amethyst cakes, pink for ruby cakes, green for emeralds, and yellow for citrines. Use a palette knife to smooth the icing onto each cake.

3 While the icing is still wet, dip and turn each cupcake in the colored crystals to get an even and encrusted layer of sparkling edible gemstones!

Makes 12 large cupcakes

candy bangles

Sticky but sweet candy bangles are fun to make and you can choose a variety of colors and flavors. A twisted spin on the traditional candy cane, you can give them as a glamorous gift or add ribbons and hang them on your Christmas tree.

You will need:
- Food coloring
- 1 cup (225g) granulated sugar
- 1 tbsp corn starch
- ½ cup (125ml) light corn syrup
- 1 tbsp butter, melted
- Few drops candy flavoring or ½ tsp vanilla extract

EQUIPMENT
- 2 nonstick lipped baking sheets
- Greased heatproof pitcher
- Candy thermometer
- Small round cookie cutter or cup

1 Preheat the oven to 225°F (110°C), Gas ¼, to keep the candy warm when you are not working it. Butter the baking sheets and put to one side for pouring the hot candy onto later. Have a greased heatproof pitcher and your food colorings to hand, as when the mix is hot enough you need to work quite quickly.

2 Put the sugar, corn starch, syrup, butter, and ½ cup (125ml) water into the pan and stir together. Heat on a medium heat until the sugar has dissolved. Clip on a candy thermometer. Bring the mix to a boil and continue to heat until it reaches 260°F (126°C), then take off the heat immediately. This takes a little time, so be patient and don't leave it unattended. For two different colors, pour half the mixture into a greased heatproof pitcher and immediately stir in the coloring and flavoring, then pour the mix onto the buttered sheet and let cool slightly. Color and flavor the remainder of the mix and pour onto the other prepared sheet. Put one batch in the oven with the door open to keep it warm.

3 Butter your hands and when the mix is not too hot to handle, pull it away from the baking sheet and begin to pull and stretch the candy.

4 Keep bringing the ends back together and continue pulling. The candy should become satiny and more opaque in appearance and become quite pliable. Repeat Steps 3-4 with the other color and keep each batch warm so that they remain workable.

5 Take one of the colored mixes and pull. Gently twist it until it starts to form a tube shape.

6 Place the candy on a flat surface and continue to roll it until it forms a long, even rope about ½in (1cm) thick. Do the same with the other colored mix so you have two ropes of roughly equal length.

tip:
Have a basin of hot water ready to put all the candy equipment in, so you can leave the pans to soak in the water to dissolve any hardened candy.

7 Take the two colored candy strands and begin to twist them around each other to make a two-toned rope. Form the bangles around a buttered mold or cutter.

8 Take your candy and pull it around the circular mold: either twist the ends round each other or trim the ends with scissors so that they meet. Continue making bangles with the rest of the candy. Keep the candy bangles stored in an airtight container on well greased paper if giving as a gift or, if using for decoration, lightly dust with corn starch to prevent them from sticking.

Makes 4 bangles

candy bangles **39**

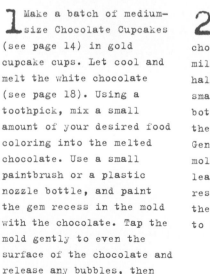

golden ring chocolate cakes

Deliciously chocolatey cupcakes topped with an edible golden, chocolate gem ring—a perfect gift for a girl or a chic treat at a tea party.

You will need:

- 1 quantity Chocolate Cupcakes (page 14)
- 4oz (100g) white chocolate
- Food coloring
- 8oz (250g) milk chocolate
- 1 quantity Rich Chocolate Buttercream (page 24)
- Edible glue
- Edible gold luster

EQUIPMENT
- Gold cupcake cups
- Toothpicks
- Small paintbrushes
- Plastic nozzle bottles
- Ring candy mold
- Small palette knife
- Waxed paper

1 Make a batch of medium-size Chocolate Cupcakes (see page 14) in gold cupcake cups. Let cool and melt the white chocolate (see page 18). Using a toothpick, mix a small amount of your desired food coloring into the melted chocolate. Use a small paintbrush or a plastic nozzle bottle, and paint the gem recess in the mold with the chocolate. Tap the mold gently to even the surface of the chocolate and release any bubbles, then refrigerate for 15 minutes.

2 While you are waiting for the colored chocolate to set, melt the milk chocolate. Transfer half the chocolate into a small pitcher or a nozzle bottle, and carefully fill the chocolate ring molds. Gently tap and return the mold to the fridge for at least 30 minutes. Leave the rest of the chocolate in the bowl or double boiler to make the buttercream.

3 Make a batch of Rich Chocolate Buttercream (see page 24). Using a small palette knife, spread each cake with the chocolate buttercream until you have a smooth surface. Take the ring mold out of the fridge and turn out the rings onto a sheet of waxed paper. Paint a thin layer of edible glue onto the milk chocolate part of the ring. Use a clean dry brush and lightly dust the rings with edible gold dust. Place a ring on top of each cupcake.

Makes 16 cupcakes

art nouveau dragonfly and butterfly cookies

Beautiful enamel-style Art Nouveau insect cookies are a perfect indulgence to adorn a table set for a splendidly sophisticated tea party.

You will need:

- 1 quantity Vanilla Cookie dough (page 16)
- 1 quantity Royal Icing (page 22)
- Food coloring in blues and greens
- Edible pearls

EQUIPMENT
- Dragonfly and butterfly cookie cutters
- 4 x No 2 icing nozzles and icing bags
- Plastic nozzle bottles

1 Preheat the oven to 325°F (160°C), Gas 3. Roll out the Vanilla Cookie dough (see page 16) and make a batch of dragonfly and butterfly shaped cookies. Separate the Royal Icing (see page 22) into three bowls and mix your blue and green colors. Spoon half of each mixture into a piping bag with nozzle. Add a few drops of water to the leftover icing until you achieve flooding consistency. Put the flooding icing into nozzle bottles.

2 Carefully pipe an outline around the edge of each cookie with different colors and let dry for about an hour.

3 Flood the cookies with the matching colored icing. Give a small tap to smooth the icing (see page 22). Let dry for at least 2 hours, preferably overnight, to make a really hard base.

4 Using the icing in the piping bags, pipe the wing details of the insects, add small edible pearls to finish off the design, and let set overnight, as you want the icing to be very hard.

Makes about 20 cookies

chocolate cameos

These beautiful chocolate cameos will make a gorgeous, tasty gift. This design is based around the classic profile of a woman in an oval frame that was popular during the reign of Queen Victoria. The molds are readily available from craft stores and online.

You will need:
- 7oz (200g) white chocolate
- 10oz (300g) milk chocolate
- Food coloring in pink and blue

EQUIPMENT
- Paintbrush
- Plastic nozzle bottles
- Cameo mold

1 Melt the white chocolate (see page 18) and let cool slightly. Use a paintbrush or nozzle bottle to paint the detail of the lady in the mold with the melted white chocolate, taking care to stay in the correct part of the pattern. Tap the mold and refrigerate for 15 minutes until the white chocolate has set.

2 Melt the milk chocolate (see page 18). Spoon the chocolate over the white painted lady to fill mold to the top. Give the mold a good tap to settle the chocolate and refrigerate for 30 minutes.

3 Remove the mold from the fridge, turn upside down, and gently tap the plastic to remove the chocolates. They will fall out easily.

Makes 16 cameos

tip:
To make pink and blue cameos, remove some of the white chocolate from the bowl and add pink or blue coloring and mix well. If you have a steady hand you can paint a little colored chocolate detail into the cameo before putting the white chocolate in. Remember to refrigerate each layer as you go.

scallop shell cookie pendants

A mermaid's medallion made from delicious vanilla cookies with a tasty marzipan pearl. Thread them onto a pretty ribbon to make a beautiful gift.

You will need:
- 1 quantity Vanilla Cookie dough (page 16)
- 2oz (50g) marzipan
- Edible pearl luster
- Edible glue or Royal Icing

EQUIPMENT
- Oyster shell cookie cutter
- Toothpicks
- Small icing nozzle
- Paintbrush
- Trim or ribbon for threading

1 Preheat the oven to 325°F (160°C), Gas 3. Roll out the Vanilla Cookie dough (see page 16) to a thickness of ¼in (3-4mm). Cut out the shell shapes and, using a toothpick, mark the indentations of the shell. Work from the middle outward to get an even pattern. Using an icing nozzle, cut out a little hole at the top of the cookies. Bake for 12-15 minutes.

2 Break off small pieces of marzipan and use your hands to roll it into little pearls about ½in (1cm) in diameter.

3 Use a dry paintbrush and gently dust the marzipan pearls with edible pearl luster. Once the cookies are cool, brush a little of the dust on the edges and into the grooves of the shell shape.

4 Dab a little edible glue or icing beneath the hole in the cookie and gently place on your pearl. Now you are ready to thread on a pretty trim or ribbon!

Makes about 18 cookies

marshmallow pearls

These beautiful and mouth-watering Marshmallow Pearls are a perfect petit four for an elegant dinner party or make a super-chic wedding favor.

You will need:

- 2 tbsp gelatin powder
- 1½ cups (300g) granulated sugar
- ¾ cup (185ml) Inverted Sugar (page 25)
- ½ cup (125ml) light corn syrup
- 1 tsp vanilla extract
- Round silicone mold
- Piping bag and nozzle
- Confectioners' (icing) sugar and corn starch
- 7oz (200g) white chocolate
- Edible pearl dust
- Paintbrush

1 Soak the gelatin in 4 tablespoons water in a mixing bowl. In a heavy bottomed saucepan, combine the sugar, a further 4 tablespoons water, and the inverted sugar. Heat but do not boil. With an electric hand-held mixer, begin to beat the gelatin and slowly add the hot syrup as it gradually combines. Slowly add the corn (golden) syrup and vanilla extract, then increase the speed to medium/high, and beat until the mixture doubles in size and becomes very fluffy and fairly stiff.

2 Butter the cavities in the silicone mold and dust each hole with a light covering of cornflour. Fill a piping bag with a ½-in (1-cm) wide nozzle with the marshmallow mix and quickly pipe into each hole in the mold. Let set for at least 1 hour (the longer the better) in a cool dry place.

3 Remove marshmallows from the mold and toss in a mixture of sifted confectioners' (icing) sugar and corn starch—this stops the mallows sticking together. Let dry for a couple of hours.

4 Melt the white
chocolate in a bowl
(see page 18) and let cool
a little. Using a fork, dip
each marshmallow into the
chocolate and gently shake
off the excess. Let cool
on a piece of waxed paper
and refrigerate until set.
Using a paintbrush, lightly
dust each marshmallow with
pearl dust.

Makes 30 marshmallows

You will need:

- 1 quantity Vanilla
  Cookie dough
  (page 16)
- 1 quantity Royal
  Icing (page 22)
- Cornflower blue
  food coloring
- ½ quantity Sugar
  Paste Icing
  (page 20)
- Edible pearls

EQUIPMENT
- Plastic nozzle bottle
- Oval cookie cutters
- 2 x no 2 icing
  nozzles and
  icing bags
- Silicone cameo mold

wedgwood cameo cookies

A delicate and elegant Wedgwood-style cameo cookie to share with ladies that lunch. These are best served with a cup of tea in a fine bone china cup and saucer—Wedgwood if possible!

1 Preheat the oven to 325°F (160°C), Gas 3. Make a batch of oval Vanilla Cookies (see page 16) and let cool. Put half of the Royal Icing (see page 22) into a bowl, color with the blue coloring, and fill a prepared piping bag with half of it. Add a few drops of water to the leftover blue icing until it reaches flooding consistency and store in a plastic nozzle bottle. Put the white icing into a piping bag for the cookie decoration.

2 Carefully pipe a blue outline around the edge of the cookies and let dry for about an hour or so. When the outline is dry, flood the cookies with blue icing, give a small tap to smooth the icing (see page 22). Let dry for at least 2 hours, preferably overnight, to make a really hard base.

3 Lightly dust the inside of the silicone mold with cornflour. Pinch off a small amount of sugar paste icing and roll it into a ball. Flatten the icing into the mold and press down. Leave in the mold for 5-10 minutes and then gently push the cameo out. Cut off any rough edges with a sharp knife to neaten the cameo.

4 Use the white icing to glue a cameo to the center of each cookie and pipe small dots in a line around the outside edge of the cookie. Pipe a line of icing around the cameo to act as glue for the edible pearls. Put a ring of pearls around the cameo and let dry completely.

Makes 20 cookies

chapter 3

Gentlemen
adorned

peppermint monocle cookies

Eccentric ginger snap and vanilla cookies with peppermint glass centers. Tie on a ribbon to make the perfect cookie for coffee dunking!

You will need:

- ½ Quantity Ginger Snap dough (page 17)
- ½ Quantity Vanilla Cookie dough (page 16)
- 7oz (200g) clear mint candies

EQUIPMENT
- Stopwatch cookie cutter
- Round cookie cutter
- ¼in (5mm) icing nozzle
- Well-greased nonstick baking sheet
- Ribbon to decorate

tip:
Don't waste the cut out circles: turn them into Button Bites (see page 56).

2 Put the mint candies into a freezer bag and smash with a rolling pin—take care as the mints will be hard, so use an old rolling pin or similar on a sturdy surface that will not mark.

1 Preheat the oven to 325°F (160°C), Gas 3. Roll out the Vanilla Cookie and Ginger Snap dough (see pages 16 and 17) on a surface lightly dusted with flour. Cut the stopwatch shapes out of the dough and then cut the centers out with a smaller circular cutter, making sure you leave a rim of at least ¼-½in (5-8mm). Use the icing nozzle to cut out a hole at the top of the monocle, this will be used to thread the ribbon. Carefully transfer the cut out shapes onto a well-greased nonstick baking sheet. Refrigerate the cookies for 5 minutes, then bake in the oven for 5 minutes until just beginning to turn golden.

3 Fill each of the cavities of the monocles with the smashed mints: don't pile them too high. Put the cookies and mint filling back into the oven for a further 5-6 minutes and watch as the mints melt. Remove from the oven and let cool for 15 minutes. With a small palette knife, gently place the cookies on a cooling rack and let cool. Tie a ribbon through each cookie to finish.
Makes about 20 cookies

button bites

Give these as gifts to your "Cute as a Button" beau. They are simple to make and fun to package: try sewing them onto a vintage-style button card or pop into little bags for the perfectly tailored gift.

You will need:

- ½ quantity Vanilla Cookie dough (page 16)
- ½ quantity Ginger Snap dough (page 17)

EQUIPMENT
- Round cookie cutters in assorted sizes
- ¼in (5mm) icing nozzle
- Palette knife
- Baking sheet

1 Preheat the oven to 325°F (160°C), Gas 3. Roll out the Vanilla Cookie and Ginger Snap dough (see pages 16 and 17) on a surface lightly dusted with flour until about ¼in (5mm) thick.

tip:
To give as gifts, thread some buttons onto a piece of card, or thread onto ribbons.

2 Use round cutters to cut out different-sized buttons. Make them quite small so that they remain cute and easy to package, I recommend between 2-3½in (5-8cm) in diameter. For each button, use the rounded end of a smaller cutter to impress an indentation to make a neat ridge.

3 Use an icing nozzle to cut two or four neat holes in each button. Push into the dough and twist slightly. Using a palette knife, lift each of the cookies onto a greased baking sheet and cool in the fridge for 5 minutes. Bake in the oven for 12-15 minutes or until just golden in color.

Makes about 35 cookies

chocolate money

Here is a great way to make money... well, the edible kind! Milk and dark chocolate money gilded with an edible golden luster make a great gift for the guys.

You will need:

- 3½oz (100g) white chocolate
- 8oz (250g) milk or dark chocolate
- Edible glue
- Edible gold luster

EQUIPMENT
- Paintbrushes
- Plastic nozzle bottle
- Chocolate coin mold
- Waxed paper

1 Melt the white chocolate (see page 18) and let cool slightly. Use a paintbrush or a nozzle bottle to fill the face on the coin with the melted white chocolate. Tap the mold gently and refrigerate for 15 minutes.

2 Melt the milk or dark chocolate as before and, using a small pitcher or a nozzle bottle, fill the coin mold and gently tap to spread the chocolate evenly. Refrigerate for at least 30 minutes.

3 Gently push out the chocolate coins onto a sheet of waxed paper. Use a paintbrush and paint a small amount of edible glue onto the coin. With a clean dry brush, gently tap on the edible gold luster.

Makes about 20 chocolates

pocket watch cookies

A distinguished gift for those who are notoriously late for dates! These delicious pocket watch cookies would make a great Father's Day gift, too. You can add a hole to the cookie and thread a ribbon through to hang as a decoration or to dip into a lovely cup of tea.

You will need:

- 1 quantity Vanilla Cookie dough (page 16)
- 1 quantity Sugar Paste Icing (page 20)
- Pocket watch cookie cutter
- Edible glue or apricot jelly (jam)
- Edible gilding medium
- Edible gold luster
- Black Royal Icing (page 22), in a piping bag with small writing nozzle
- Small gold dragees

EQUIPMENT
- Baking sheet
- Paintbrushes
- Round cookie cutter

1 Preheat the oven to 325°F (160°C), Gas 3. Roll out the Vanilla Cookie dough (see page 16) on a lightly floured surface to an even thickness of ¼in (3–4mm). Cut out the pocket watch shapes and transfer to a greased baking sheet. Refrigerate for 10 minutes, then bake for 12–15 minutes. Let cool.

2 Dust the work surface with confectioners' (icing) sugar or corn starch and roll out the Sugar Paste Icing to a thickness of about ¼in (3mm) and cut out the watch shapes. Take a round cutter that is smaller than the outside of the watch, and using the blunt side make an indentation on the face of the watch.

3 Paint a small amount of edible glue onto the cookie. If you don't have any glue you can warm up some apricot jelly (jam) and use that instead.

4 Carefully lift the icing pieces and place them on the sticky surface of the cookie. Press gently into place.

6 Use the piping bag of black royal icing and ice around the circumference of the cookie by filling in the indented line.

5 Paint a thin layer of edible gilding medium around the outside of the cookie. Use a small, dry paintbrush to gently dust the edge of the cookie with gold luster.

7 Starting at the 12 o'clock position, carefully pipe bars to represent the numbers on a clock face. If you prefer and have a steady hand, you could pipe the actual numbers instead.

8 Starting at the center of the watch face, ice a small line for the hour hand followed by a longer line for the minute hand. Draw a little arrow head at the end of each line and place a small dot in the the center of the watch where the two lines meet.

9 Finally, place a small gold dragee in the center of the watch, pressing it carefully in place with a toothpick.

Makes about 20 cookies

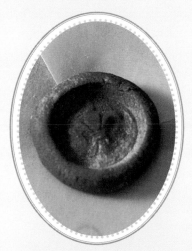

fondant seals

The ultimate food lover's correspondence card! These stamped fondant seals are great for a personalized gift—you can use any stamp and then stick the seal to a totally edible rice paper envelope.

You will need:
- Scant 2 cups (250g) confectioners' (icing) sugar
- ¼ tsp cream of tartar
- 1 egg white, lightly whisked
- 4 tbsp light (single) cream
- Red food coloring
- Strawberry flavoring
- Royal Icing (page 22)

EQUIPMENT
- Patterned stamp
- Waxed paper
- 5 sheets rice paper

1 Sift the confectioners' (icing) sugar and cream of tartar into a mixing bowl. Slowly mix in the egg white and cream and stir well until combined. Add a few drops of strawberry flavoring and red food coloring and knead into a dough. Add more confectioners' sugar if it is too sticky. Sift some confectioners' sugar onto a board and turn out the fondant. Continue to knead until the color is even and the dough is pliable. Wrap in plastic wrap (cling film) and leave for an hour.

2 Pinch off a small amount of the fondant and roll into a ball; dip your stamp into some confectioners' sugar and indent into the fondant ball. Let dry on a sheet of waxed paper.

3 Cut a rectangle and a triangle out of rice paper. Ice together with Royal Icing to make a small envelope and ice on the fondant seal to close.

Makes about 20 seals

chapter 4

Celebration
gifts

cherub cakes

A celestial treat... a gilded cherub atop a striking and delicious cupcake is the perfect seaonal touch for a Christmas party, or a beautiful gift to take to loved ones over the festive period.

You will need:

- ½ quantity Vanilla Cupcakes (page 13)
- 10oz (300g) white chocolate
- 1 quantity Buttercream Icing (page 23)
- ½ tsp almond essence
- Turquoise food coloring
- Edible glue
- Edible gold luster

EQUIPMENT
- Gold cupcake cups
- Pitcher or plastic nozzle bottle
- Cherub mold
- Toothpicks
- Piping bag with ½in (1cm) rope nozzle
- Small paintbrush

1 Halving the quantities in the recipe on page 13, make a batch of six Vanilla Cupcakes using gold cupcake cups in a large muffin pan. While the cakes are cooling, melt the white chocolate (see page 18) and let cool a little. Transfer the chocolate into a pitcher or a plastic nozzle bottle. Fill each cavity of the cherub mold and gently tap to release any bubbles. Put the mold in the fridge and let the chocolate set for at least 1 hour.

2 Add the almond essence to the Buttercream Icing (see page 23). Use a toothpick to add some food coloring to the icing. Mix thoroughly to obtain an even, rich color. Fill a piping bag with the icing and ice the top of each cupcake in a circular pattern.

3 Take the cherubs out of the fridge and turn them out onto a sheet of waxed paper by gently pressing around the shapes on the back of the mold. Use a paintbrush to paint a small amount of edible glue all over the surface of the cherubs. Using a clean, dry brush gently dab each angel with gold luster. To finish, place a golden cherub on top of each cupcake.

Makes 6 large cupcakes

stained glass cookies

These stained-glass style snowflake cookies can be made in a rainbow of festive colors and look beautiful hung in a window to catch the light—the perfect edible Christmas decoration.

You will need:

- 1 quantity Vanilla Cookie dough (page 16)
- 1 package boiled candies in assorted colors

EQUIPMENT
- Well-greased nonstick baking sheet
- Snowflake cookie cutter set
- Toothpicks
- Icing nozzle
- Small palette knife
- Ribbon for hanging

1 Preheat the oven to 325°F (160°C), Gas 3. Roll out the Vanilla Cookie dough (see page 16) on a lightly floured surface to ¼in (3-4mm) thickness. Transfer to a well-greased nonstick baking sheet. It's easier to cut out the detail on the cookies on the sheet, as they will be too delicate to move later. Cut out the snowflake shapes and then, using the small insert cutters, cut out snowflake patterns. Remove any stubborn pieces of dough with a toothpick. Use the icing nozzle to cut out a hole at the top of the snowflake; this will be used to thread the ribbon. Put the cookies in the fridge for 10 minutes and then part-bake the cookies for 6 minutes. Let cool on the baking sheet.

2 Put the boiled candies into separate sealed bags according to colors and smash with a rolling pin. Take care as the sweets will be hard, so use an old rolling pin or similar on a sturdy surface that will not mark.

3 Fill each of the snowflake cavities with pieces of smashed candy. Don't pile them too high. Pop the cookies back into the oven for a further 5-6 minutes. Remove from the oven. The "glass" parts will be bubbly, but the bubbles disappear as they cool. Leave the snowflakes on the sheet to cool for at least 20 minutes. With a small palette knife, gently slide under the cookies and lift each one off the sheet and let cool on a cooling rack. Tie each cookie with a ribbon to hang on your tree. Makes 12 cookies

rosette cookies

Say "Happy Birthday" or "Congratulations" with these rosette cookies. Decorated with vibrant fondant icing, you can finish off with any number or letter that's fitting for the celebration.

You will need:

- 1 quantity Ginger Snap dough (page 17)
- Sugar Paste Icing (page 20 or readymade)
- Food coloring
- Corn starch
- Edible glue or apricot jelly (jam)

EQUIPMENT
- Rosette cookie cutter
- Baking sheet
- Paintbrushes
- Palette knife
- Garrett frill cutter
- Round or fluted cutters
- Toothpicks
- Number and letter cutters

1 Preheat the oven to 325°F (160°C), Gas 3. Roll out the Ginger Snap dough (see page 17) on a lightly floured surface and cut into rosette shapes. Transfer onto a greased baking sheet. Bake in the oven for 15–20 minutes. Let cool. Color your Sugar Paste Icing (see page 20) in your chosen colors. Lightly dust your work surface with corn starch and roll out the icing to about ⅛in (2–3mm) thickness. Cut out using the rosette cutter.

2 Paint edible glue onto the top surface of each cookie, or melt a little apricot jelly (jam) in a pan and use that instead.

3 With a palette knife, carefully put the sugar-paste rosette base on top of the cookie.

Makes 12 cookies

4 To make the frilly ribbon, use either a garrett frill cutter or a simple round cutter a little smaller than the round part of the cookie. Use corn starch to dust your surface and roll out a contrasting color of sugar paste to about ⅛in (2mm) thickness. Cut out the shape.

5 Using a toothpick, carefully roll the edges of the icing to thin them out and make a frill shape. Repeat Steps 4–5 to make a second frill.

6 Paint the sugar paste topping with edible glue and put the frill or circle in place. Repeat to add another frilly layer.

7 Use a small round cutter to cut out the center of the rosette and cut out a number or letter. You could handpaint onto the rosette using edible inks or food colorings, too. Use edible glue to secure the center pieces in place.

Makes about 12 cookies

fabergé-style easter cookies

Fabergé eggs have always been a symbol of opulent extravagance and these delicious cookies are inspired by the intricate creations that delighted the Russian tsars. Decorate them with colored frosting and edible pearls and give them as the perfect Easter gift.

You will need:

- 1 quantity Vanilla Cookie dough (page 16)
- 1 quantity Royal Icing (page 22)
- Food coloring in assorted pastel colors
- Edible pearls

EQUIPMENT
- Egg shape cookie cutters
- Baking sheet
- 3 x No 2 icing nozzles and icing bags

1 Preheat the oven to 325°F (160°C), Gas 3. Roll out the Vanilla Cookie dough (see page 16) on a lightly floured surface and cut into egg shapes. Place on a greased baking sheet. Bake in the oven for 12–15 minutes. Prepare a batch of Royal Icing (see page 22) in several colors. Remove half of each quantity of icing and transfer into separate bowls for flooding (see page 22). Mix each color with a few drops of water until they are the consistency of light cream.

2 Carefully pipe an outline around the edge of the cookies and let dry for about an hour, before flooding the cookie with the watered-down icing. Give a small tap to smooth the icing (see page 22). Let the cookies dry for at least 2 hours, preferably overnight, to make a really hard base.

3 Using the colored icing in the piping bags, apply your Fabergé-style pattern onto the cookies, following the picture opposite as a guide.

4 Add small edible pearls to finish the cookies and let set overnight, as you want the icing to be very hard before packaging.

Makes about 30 cookies

4 Smooth the marzipan over and around the cakes and trim off any excess at the base of the cake.

5 Roll out the Sugar Paste Icing to ⅛in (2mm) thick. Cut out circles as before to cover each cake. Paint a little water onto the marzipan to act as glue. Cover each cake with the sugar paste, smooth over, and trim any excess. Keep the sugar paste covered with plastic wrap (cling film) when you are not working with it, to prevent it from drying out. To make a base for the bottom cake, cut out a circle from the sugar paste using the 2½in (6cm) cutter. Use a small amount of jelly (jam) to stick the base onto the cake.

6 Dust the inside of the bead trim maker with edible pearl luster, roll a small coil of Sugar Paste Icing (see page 20) the same length as the maker and place it into the pearl grooves, close, and gently pull out your string of indented pearls. Trim any excess icing off the pearls.

7 Using Royal Icing (see page 22), pipe the bottom of the smaller cake and place on top of the base cake to make your two tiers. Cut pieces of ribbon to place around the bottom and middle of the cakes. Use a small amount of Royal Icing to glue the ribbons in place and to secure the overlapped ends. Using a small amount of Royal Icing, secure the pearls in place around the middle of the cake.

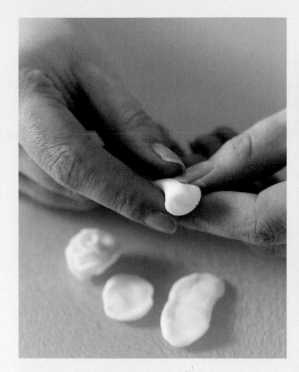

9 Dust the roses with a little edible pearl luster and cut off the bottom of the rose to make a neat base. Using royal icing, glue the rose on top of the cake.

Makes 4 cakes

8 To make small sugar paste roses, pinch off a small amount of icing, flatten it between your forefinger and thumb, and coil up to make the spiral center of a rose. Pinch off two more pieces and flatten out with your thumb, wrap one petal around the center of the rose. Use your fingers to shape the petals. Repeat with the other petal. Keep the petals covered with plastic wrap to prevent them from drying out.

tip:
Try adding a little food coloring to the Royal Icing to make cakes and decorative detailing in a range of different colors.

golden jelly hearts

Divinely romantic juicy jelly hearts are set with real edible gold leaf. A very luxurious and fruity treat for your loved one to finish a passionate Valentine's feast!

You will need:

- 2 sheets fine leaf gelatin
- Scant ½ cup (100ml) clear lemonade
- 2 sheets edible gold leaf
- 4 tbsp pomegranate juice

EQUIPMENT
- Bain marie
- Heart-shaped candy molds

1 Cut up one sheet of gelatin and soak in a little of the lemonade for 10 minutes in a glass bowl.

2 Add the rest of the lemonade to the bowl and gently heat over a pan of simmering water or in a bain marie, until the gelatin has fully dissolved.

3 Let the mixture cool and refrigerate until it starts to thicken slightly, but so it can still easily be poured. Take the mix out of the refrigerator and whisk in the gold leaf to break it up into lots of pieces that will sit throughout the gel shape. If the gel has not thickened slightly, the gold leaf will sink.

4 Pour a small amount of the golden gel mixture into the bottom of each heart mold and refrigerate until set.

5 Make the pomegranate jelly. Mix the juice and 4 tablespoons water together. Cut the remaining leaf of gelatin up as before. Soak the gelatin in a little of the juice and water and leave for 10 minutes, then add the rest of the juice and continue as in Step 2. Let the gel mix cool down completely before pouring onto the set gold layer in the molds. Leave in the fridge until completely set.

tip:
You can add a tiny bit of red food coloring to the juice to enhance the color if you wish.

6 To turn out the jelly hearts, place the base of the mold in a shallow dish of warm water to loosen the hearts and then turn upside down on a plate and tap to release.

Makes 6 small hearts

engagement cookies

These sparkling engagement ring cookies make the perfect bridal favor or engagement gifts. Tie with a beautiful ribbon around a napkin to make a stunning table decoration.

You will need:

- 1 quantity Vanilla Cookie dough (page 16)
- 1 quantity Sugar Paste Icing (page 20)
- Edible glue
- Edible gilding medium
- Edible gold luster

EQUIPMENT
- Diamond ring cookie cutter
- Small round cookie cutter
- Small paintbrushes
- Toothpick

3 Use a toothpick to mark indentations of the diamond and the ring setting.

1 Preheat the oven to 325°F (160°C), Gas 3. Make a batch of ring-shaped Vanilla Cookies (see page 20), cutting the center of the ring with a small cutter Let cool. Dust the work surface with confectioners' (icing) sugar and roll out the Sugar Paste Icing to a thickness of about ⅛in (2mm). Cut out the ring shapes and the center of the ring again with a round cutter.

2 Paint a small amount of edible glue, or warmed apricot jelly (jam), onto the cookies, lift the icing pieces, and press them gently into place.

4 Paint a thin layer of edible gilding medium around the outside of the cookie, leaving the diamond. If the medium is a little hard, just remove a small amount from the pot onto a plate and mix it slightly to warm it up. Take a small dry paintbrush and using edible gold luster, gently dust the edge and the setting of the ring.

Makes 18 cookies

halloween sugar skulls

These crystal sugar skulls are fantastic served to sweeten a bitter hot chocolate on a scary winter's day. The skulls can also be made to celebrate the Mexican Day of the Dead—just adorn with bright colored icing.

You will need:
- 1⅓ cups (250g) superfine (caster) sugar
- 1 tsp meringue powder
- Black royal icing in a piping bag (page 22), with No 2 piping nozzle
- Edible diamonds and pearls

EQUIPMENT
- Skull candy mold
- Waxed paper
- Baking sheet

1 Put the sugar in a mixing bowl and mix with the meringue powder. Add one teaspoon water and mix together with your hands—the mixture will feel like damp sand. The sugar is ready when your hands leave an imprint if you squeeze the sugar.

2 Pack the sugar down tightly into the skull mold with a spoon.

3 Place a piece of waxed paper onto a flat baking sheet and hold tightly over the mold. When you flip the skulls over, make sure you have a good grip on the mold and the baking sheet.

4 Gently lift off the mold and leave the skulls to dry for at least 4 hours or overnight.

5 Use your black icing to carefully pipe details of the eyes, nose, and teeth on the skulls.

6 Press edible pearls and diamonds into the icing to make spooky-looking eyes.

Makes 16 sugar skulls

chapter 5

Fun
for
children

2 For marshmallows and gummy sweets, take a lace and flatten the end with a small rolling pin until it is thin enough to thread through the eye of a large darning needle.

3 Thread the marshmallows and sweets in whatever order you like, leaving enough room at the ends to make a knot to secure. Now wear, eat, and enjoy!

cherry garland necklace

A childhood movie theater favorite—Cherry Candies! You can make this beautiful garland necklace with a few easy knots. Then take yourself to the movies and munch away!

You will need:
- 8 cherry-shaped gummy candies
- 6 green candy strings
- 4 red strawberry laces

1 Lay the cherries in a line so that the colors match, red to red and green to green. Make sure that there is a green stalk at both ends of the line.

2 Take a section of green string and tie on the first stalk with a reef knot. To do this, cross the right end over the left end and pull under, then cross the left end over the right end and pull under. Pull both ends tight and trim the ends to neaten. Repeat this where pairs of green stalks meet.

3 To make the links to join the red cherries together, repeat the knot in Step 2, using sections of the red laces.

4 Take one long length of the green string and feed it through both ends of the cherry chain and tie in a reef knot, trimming the ends to neaten. Pull the string through so it doubles up to create the cord for the back of the necklace.

Makes 1 necklace

candy cocktail rings

Bling bling cocktail rings are so much fun to make, wear, and eat! You can adorn your table with bowls of retro candies and sprinkles and create your own concoctions, a great idea for childrens' parties.

You will need:

- Candy laces or fruit strings
- Lifesaver candies and hard candy rings
- Small bonbons
- Fruit candies (Mentos or similar)
- Colored sugar
- Sprinkles and sugar pearls
- ½ quantity Royal Icing (page 22) in a piping bag

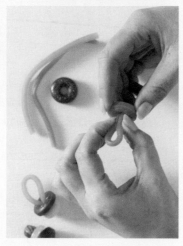

1 Cut a length of lace long enough to go around a finger, plus ¾in (2cm). Make a loop and pinch the ends together, then feed the ends into the center of a candy with a hole.

2 Pipe a small dot of Royal Icing to act as glue to hold the lace in place and let dry. This will form the ring base.

3 To make a hard candy gem ring, pipe a dot of Royal Icing around the center hole. Press on a smaller ring candy, making sure it is stuck securely. Pipe a dot of Royal Icing into the center and attach a small hard candy gem.

4 To make an encrusted ring, take the ring base made in Step 2 and pipe a dot of Royal Icing around the center hole. Press on a round candy or bonbon and let dry for a few minutes.

5 Pipe Royal Icing onto the top of the candy, and spread the icing so the whole of the top surface is covered. Dip the sticky iced ring into a bowl of sprinkles or colored sugar to create the encrusted look.

tip:
You can also use multiple hard candies and sugar pearls to glamorous effect!

cookie charm necklaces

These fun and colorful cookie necklaces are a huge favorite with children; they can be made with countless playful shapes, colors, and flavors.

You will need: ○

- Food coloring
- 1 quantity Vanilla Cookie dough (page 16)
- Flavoring (optional)

EQUIPMENT
- Assorted cookie cutters
- ¼in (4mm) icing nozzle
- Palette knife
- Baking sheets
- Selection of ribbons

1 Preheat the oven to 275°F (140°C), Gas 1. Make a batch of colored Vanilla Cookie dough (see page 16). On a floured surface roll out your dough to a thickness of ¼in (4mm).

2 Cut out the cookies using various shapes of cutters. Use a ¼in (4mm) piping nozzle to cut out the holes that you will use to thread the cookies. Twist the nozzle slightly to cut out an even hole. Using a palette knife, gently put the cookies onto baking sheets, refrigerate for 5 minutes, and then bake for 18–20 minutes. Keep a close eye on the cookies to make sure that they don't brown.

3 Leave the cookies on a cooling rack until cool and then thread onto ribbons to make necklaces.

Makes 40 cookie charms

rice paper blossom jewels

These delicate-looking flowers are so easy to make. Either ice them onto ribbons or edible laces and wear them, or just use them as amazing cake toppers.

You will need:

- 10 sheets colored and white rice paper
- Edible pearls
- Royal Icing (page 22), in a piping bag
- Ribbons or edible laces

EQUIPMENT
- Scissors and flower template or flower punches

1 Cut out flowers shapes in different sizes and colors. You can either use a flower template or cookie cutter to draw around or craft punches. There are lots of shapes and sizes of flower punches available.

2 Take one large flower and using Royal Icing pipe dots around its edges and the center. Secure an edible lace (or ribbon, if using) in the center and place a second large flower on top of this. Press down to secure and leave to dry for a few minutes. Repeat this method to iceg on more layers of flowers in contrasting shapes and sizes.

3 Using the icing, pipe a little dot into the middle of the flower and attach an edible pearl.

index

I would like to say a HUGE
thank you to my wonderful Thomas
for all his love, support, encouragement, and
new-found candy-making skills.

To my amazing Mum, from whom I have inherited the
creative baking gene and all the home-making skills
a woman could need.

To Eleanor Bolton who has been my right-hand woman
and discovered an amazing untapped skill for making
jewelry out of candies!

To Dad, James, and Teddy for being their
wonderful selves.

To Stuart West for the amazing photography and for being
so brilliant and such fun to work with.

To Kate Wilson for her beautiful illustrations that
keep me inspired.

To the Team at Cico for all their help
and support.

The publisher would like to thank Thornback and Peel for
providing the jelly mold motif wallpaper
used for some style-shot backgrounds.
www.thornbackandpeel.co.uk